Sunshine On The Dewdrop

A Collection of Poetic Reflections

Shraddha Bhat

BookLeaf Publishing

India | USA | UK

Made with ❤ on the BookLeaf Publishing Platform
www.bookleafpub.in
www.bookleafpub.com

Dedication

I dedicate this book to-

My mother **Pratibha Joshi**, from whom I inherited this gift of writing and reflection, who herself is an accomplished and published poet and writer.

and,

My father **Chandrakant Joshi**, who although an engineer by profession, has a keen interest in literature.

I am eternally grateful to both of you for encouraging me to keep writing.

Preface

"Poetry is when an emotion has found its thought and the thought has found words." -- Robert Frost.

Poetry is an intense emotion that is expressed coherently... an imagination, a thought, caught in beautiful words. I have been an avid reader and admirer of poetry since childhood. My mother being a poet has shaped my love for poetic expressions and my love for beauty in nature and all things in life.

Having an interest in poetry, be it as a poet or as an admirer of poetry, definitely elevates the experience of life. Observing nature, pondering over ideas and expressing your imaginations gives a pure joy to the heart, mind and soul.

In this collection of pocms I have expressed my observations and reflections about nature and life. I have reflected upon different emotions and ideas in these poems. I hope you will enjoy reading them as I have enjoyed writing them.

Acknowledgements

It was a fortunate stroke of serendipity that I came across Bookleaf Publishing Company. Because of their writing challenge, I was able to push myself to go beyond my comfort zone and pen down my reflections.

I am grateful to Bookleaf Publishing Company for inspiring a poet like me to write consistently by giving the opportunity to publish my work. I am much obliged to the team of Bookleaf Publishing Company and their help desk for their assistance and guidance during the compiling and editing process. I am grateful to Amazon for publishing paperback copies of this book.

I am indebted to Ms. Wendy Stickney Klatt, MAT, an English language educator, for proofreading my poems and offering valuable suggestions and insights. I sincerely appreciate the encouragement and support she provided me. I am grateful to my sister Deepti Janorkar for providing meaningful feedback, motivating me to write, and supporting me in any endeavor I take on. Many thanks to my nieces, Sanika Janorkar and Aabha Bhat, for reading my poems and for cheering me on. I am indebted to my family, extended family, and friends for encouraging me to keep writing.

I appreciate the steadfast support of my husband Jaideep Bhat. I am grateful to him for being the first reader and critic of these, and all my poems, and for offering his insights. Lastly, and most of all, I appreciate my son Shreyas for being there for me and inspiring me all the time.

And above all, I am truly grateful to you, dear readers. I hope you like these reflections.

Warm regards,

Shraddha Bhat

Sunshine On The Dewdrop

Dew clung to the grass blades
Swinging carefree, that misty morning
When mysterious hues of gray and pinkish gold
Were shifting in the sky.

And the dewdrop
Watched its secretive play,
Expecting wonders.

The heavy curtain of fog was lifted
By numerous golden hands of sun
And in that magic moment,
The dewdrop glowed
Taking in all the sunshine,
Holding the entire image of that radiance
In its heart.

That tiny golden bead
Dazzled with shear joy,
Pure light.

As mysteriously as it came into being,
It evaporated.

Isn't it breathtaking, though?
The insignificant, ephemeral existence
Made mesmerizingly beautiful by
Being the vessel of light!

Snowflakes

They descended secretly in the inky blue night,
Snowflakes -

or

Frozen whispers from the stars?

Weaving a shimmering veil of dreams and reality,
They carried moonlight on their intricately patterned
wings,
Scattering crystalized moonbeams on the earth.

When the sky turned shades of purple and pale pink,
And then luminous scarlet gold,
They continued daintily drifting down -
A gossamer of glistening sunshine.
And transformed into a soft, velvety, glittering drape
Enveloping all,
Magically smoothing over
The jagged, rugged edges of the crude terrain
With its enchanting gentle touch.

The Mirage Of Life

Clear, blue, cold skies
An almost non-existent breeze.
It is so hopelessly still -
Silence overwhelming,
Echoing in all directions

Do you feel an edge to this stillness?
An arrow tensely stretched on a bow,
Something waiting to unleash?

The sun is exceptionally bright
Its rays slam into
Crisp, glittering snowscape,
Refracting a pearly glare

It seems another dimension,
An alien universe.

Bitter chill seeps into the heart, numbing senses.
Hopes frostbitten,

Dreams silent in the haze of emptiness.

Was it here that life once flourished?
Birds sang? Flowers bloomed?
And trees swayed with pride and glee?
Is it a distant memory from another lifetime?
Was that a fantasy, or this an illusion?

How could one be sure
If this pristine, unblemished, flawless white snow-desert,
Intensely longing to melt into a murky green mess,
Is fate's design waiting to unfold?
Or
Do you merely see
The Mirage of Life on the Horizon?

Spring

I woke up to this sweet alluring call
My alarm last season, I fondly recall
I so missed this chirpy bird song,
And my heart hummed along.
The sun shone warmer, the sky a little clearer,
And the grass was a shade greener.

The air was expectant,
The trees were impatient
To burst into exuberance,
The pure joy of delicate blossoms.

Now,
The monochrome nature will transform
Into a vibrant color scheme.
The birds will soar to sky and sing
Songs of a joyous theme.
Hummingbirds will hum, butterflies will flutter,
Emulating miniature suns, yellow dandelions will glitter
The frozen hopes will begin to sprout,

My heart cried out -
Behold, the magic is about to begin,
Spring is coming.

Summer On The Beach

Foam topped waves of azure
Keep crashing on the shore,
Etched in my heart are
Memories of beaches and summer.

Soothing hues of cyan seashores,
Warm sun, cool breezes,
Innumerable shades of gold and blue.

And in the distance,
Where ocean flaunts its deep azure, silky drape
With its sun-gold embroidered shimmer,
Clear blue sky peers into a vast, deep mirror.
Pleased by its own reflection,
It tries on a myriad of moods and colors -
Coral pink dawns and the sunsets tangerine,
Splashes of scarlet and clouds with silver linings.

Beaches dotted with colorful sea glass, pearly seashells
The touch of moist, soft sand on the feet,

Warm sun on the face.
Caresses of salt-kissed, silky breezes,
Aroma of deep ocean and seaweed.

Vivid visions keep flashing in my mind's eye -
Just as rhythmically, incessantly as the waves
As they gently crash at my feet.

And I eagerly wait for summer on the beach,
Where gold and tranquil cyan meet,
On such sandy shores, I long to walk bare feet.

Fabric Of Life

One keeps on knitting,
The fabric of life.
With the threads of sorrows and joys,
Light and shadows.

And in turn, life weaves
Our identity.

You grow, you stumble,
Fail and rise again,
And repeat it a thousand times.

A part of you dies and is born renewed,
With mesmerizing colors,
And a completely alien design.
Life can grow so puzzling sometimes.

Some patterns re-emerge,
Some threads run deep.
Memories are forgotten, words wither, hurts fade,

But the wisdom stays -
As a core, that sustains us.

This fabric,
A tapestry of coincidences and serendipity -
May it be plain or delicately embroidered,
What is essential is that we are
Wrapped in it, warm and snug.
Then, life can grow delightful sometimes.

Change Is Constant

Moments come, moments go.
What was new is now old.

Dawns rise, suns set,
Days surreptitiously change fate.
Shadows emerge in fading light,
The skies evolve with every night.

Seconds run, eons pass -
Nothing slips through Time's grasp.

Unending spools of unravelling time,
Infinite threads of possibilities sublime.

Unless we become aware and conscious,
This dance of life and force may baffle us.

Mountains will erode, galaxies will vanish,
From absolute nothing, exuberance will flourish.

Shifting imageries and drifting dreams,
Transmuting dramas and changing scenes -
Ceaselessly flowing, nothing is stagnant.
In the flux called Universe, only change is constant.

A Walk To Peace

It was so quiet, so still
That dreary afternoon
Just the gentle whisper of wind
Birds paused their songs
Until the sun sets...

This dull quiet was a stark contrast to the
Deafening Chaos in my mind,
A cacophony of conflicting ideas and ideals
A tsunami of emotions,
Incessant worry
Again and again it circled back to pain.

The turmoil inside grew unbearable
I stepped out to walk
The overlapping, overwhelming noise outside
Surprisingly soothed.
The meandering path took me to
A discreetly hidden meadow
With numerous shades of green.

The wind was gentle, and sunbeams golden
Daffodils stole sunshine from the source
Grass embroidered delicate green around the lake.
Trees donned moss colored stockings
Clear blue skies, dotted with tweeting birds
And occasional cotton candy clouds
Silky fragrant breezes.

All my worries evaporated, agony vanished
This unassuming beauty, tranquility
Percolated through my being
Peace enveloped and engulfed me
So completely, I disappeared
Into the blue lucid serenity!!

Dichotomy

A feather that drifts in the wind,
Or a minuscule particle of sand
In an hour-glass,
Constantly shifting and slipping
Escaping the clutches of time eternal,
That's how I feel sometimes
Disconnected, untethered, free
Although... just for a strange blissful moment.
But that is enough to breathe in new hopes
In my dreary, anchored existence.

The next moment,
I am back to my secured reality,
Pinpointing my place,
Firmly tethered to its coordinates,
To the four-dimensional constructs of my identity.
As a fixed small cross-stitch
In the rich embroidered tapestry of life.
A predestined pattern,
A precise, concise point, concretely embedded in my

reality!

Perhaps, it's not so rigid and fixed as I wearily perceive?
But a tightly wound seed
With enumerable unexplored possibilities?

Firmly secured in the soil of existence
In search of nourishing, soothing touch of water
Will it go deeper, anchoring itself to the Earth?
Or will it seek its strong affinity to the azure in the sky?
Its thirst for the golden light?

Will it balance this dichotomy
Its inherent urge for security,
And its insistent hope to be free?

Rainbow

As a portal between heaven and earth,
Dreams and reality,
Spanning the two worlds -
The rainbow shone radiantly,
The celestial gift.

The luminous greenery below,
And translucent blue above -
An arc connecting real to ethereal.

A glimmer of iridescence
Sparkling on the lakes.
And when shimmering droplets
Fall from the trees,
When the sun-gold meets the diamond drops of rain,
Vivid colors burst forth.

When the vision is met with grace,
The spectrum of possibilities emerges,
And a rainbow is born.

Joy

An effervescence
Or luminous exuberance -
What is joy, really?

Is it as fleeting as the caress of a gentle breeze?
Or is it as everlasting as the brilliant sun?
Overshadowed by an array of clouds?

When the morning sun kisses our face,
When flowers bloom
When bluebirds unexpectedly land
Near you from their high perch,
When a baby tightly clasps your finger and heart,
When a long forgotten memory pleasantly surprises -

In these blissful instances,
Did joy visit momentarily,
Like a butterfly visiting a flower?
Or was joy always there?
High above, or deep within,

Shadowed by mundane things
And routine patterns of thoughts?

Or do you feel delight at those beautiful interludes,
Because your heart soars, soul rises to its peak
To be one with eternal luminous joy?

Dawn

The day broke as a whisper,
Awakening nature from its tender dream.
Star-studded black veil of the night sky
Transformed into a translucent gossamer of misty fog.

Horizon emerged from the twilight,
Applying a thin line of light as kohl.
The sky blushed with coral purple pink hues.
The symphony of bird songs,
Reached its crescendo.
Trees glowed with sunshine,
Flowers offered fragrance to the gentle breeze.
Every grass blade and tender petal
Was showered with pearls of dew.

Golden dewdrops giggled mischievously,
Holding images of sun in their bellies.
Nature unfolded a carpet of velvety grass,
Countless flowers bloomed.
Thus was the majestic welcome offered to the dawn.

Memories

When I rest my eyes after a long day,
A cascade of old memories come knocking
On my heart.

And I can feel the glow upon my closed eyes -
Of the light that once streamed through the weave of
leaves.
I can feel the dense, cooling shadows of mango trees
On hot summer days,
Lingering fragrance of the mangoes,
And a deliciously sweet taste on my tongue.

I still remember -
The caress of warm gentle rain on my face,
The soft touch of delicate coral lilies in my palms,
Sweet calls of the nightingales.

Vibrant colors,
In the gardens and the bazaars,
Bright sunny days and starlit nights,

Drifting off to sleep on the terrace,
Watching the falling stars.

Holy basil in its decorated pot
In the backyard,
And a quiet oil lamp burning beside it,
Giving serenity to the already tranquil evenings.

Simple were the days then,
Simpler the wishes.

After the busy day was over,
All we needed was
Mother's hopeful stories of princesses and fairies,
And her voice still echoing in our dreams
As we drifted off to sleep.

Love

The gentle curve of your smile,
A luminous crescent moon,
Lights up my shadowy heart.

I love how your smile reaches your eyes
And sometimes,
When you find humor in mundane things,
Only your eyes smile.

Your heartbeat, A soothing melody
Instantly calms my weary soul.

The lilting tone of your voice,
When you share your day,
Is honey in my ears.

The sound of your laughter,
Random tunes that you hum,
Keeps echoing in my mind
Like a silent song, a harmony.

I think of you when I hear a beautiful song,
When I come up with witty anecdotes,
And when an old, vivid memory suddenly pops up.
You are always there - in presence or thoughts.

A shared dream beckons us,
A common hope moves us.

I feel quiet whispers of your heart -
You pervade my existence.
You are unquestionably,
An indivisible part of me.

When we took each other's hand,
Our heartlines, our lifelines merged.
Our fates intertwined.

Call it Love, call it a delightful Destiny -
There is no other way, there is no other life.
With you by my side, everything is right.

Sacred Bond

Hope gleams in your expressive eyes
And shadows of pain.
O my blueberry-eyed sweet boy,
Your smile - purity with no stain.

Without you uttering a word,
I can hear hymns of your soul,
Feel the rhythm of your heart
Perceive your essence, your truth whole.

I remember when I first saw you,
A flickering smile on lips, eyes tight shut
Tiny fist tightly clutching my finger
With such pure trust.

From that sweet moment -
You have forever clasped my heart.
Your innocent love, unshakable trust,
For this sacred bond, I live, I exist.

Let you always be secure, nestled in care,
Let there be no empty nest for me to endure.

27

Illusion

One evening in autumn,
I sat mesmerized
At the foot of a maple tree,
Watching the splashes of crimson
Where sky met the earth
At the glowing horizon.
Birds gliding, bathed in the glow of sky
I wish I could join them, I could fly.

A gentle breeze rustling my unruly hair,
About to engulf me was the gray of dispair.
From their perch on high branches
Gently landed beside me, a pair of goldfinches.
On the carpet of red and gold leaves,
I sat under a wishing tree, I believe.

Complete was the beautiful illusion,
Or my wish came to fruition?
Scarlet and gold beaneth me and up high,
As if, with the goldfinches I was flying in the sky.

Inspiration

Inspired visions shower,
Drop by drop,
Ever so lightly.

They trickle down
Into the heart, into the soul
Taking the mood of the heart,
And the color of the soul.

Flow through the veins,
They percolate -
In dreams, in thoughts,
In imagination,
And unfold in a myriad of expressions,
Just as a cherry tree blossoms in spring.
Giving a unique shimmer
To my mundane existence.

Yearning

A tender, tiny seedling,
Tightly wound.
With hidden possibilities of
Magnificence -
Unknown to itself.

It silently hums the songs of the future,
Believing in its core,
In its untapped potential.

It yearns intensely
For the illuminating light,
To breathe in the free air,
While still buried in the suffocating obscurity.

And with all its might,
It pushes through the weight of dense soil,
Anchoring itself firmly,
Reaching into the depths of inert rocky earth.

Against the heavy burden of the fate,
It rises above the oppressing dark,
To drink the golden elixir of sunshine.

Serendipity

Wherever I go, whomever I meet,
These chance encounters are always a treat.

Whenever I dance to life's strange beat,
Fate tries to join in with two left feet.

Taking in the wonder, whenever I breathe,
Surreptitiously spring memories discrete.

I remember the smile and moments sweet,
That laughter still echoes in my heartbeat.

Treasured are the songs and melodies elite,
Such strange serendipity does seldom repeat.

Pond

I walk to the pond
Nestled in the forest beyond.
To calm my heart in its blue serenity,
To experience its pristine clarity.
To soothe my soul,
To mend my fragmented self whole.
I don't have wings to fly,
How can I reach the blue expanse up high?
So I go to the pond to see,
In the image of sky, the reflection of me.

Autumn

The forest was ablaze
With yellow, red and orange
Flickering flames,
The wind was blowing
Flamboyant leaves rustling fervently.
Leaf 'n leaf,
Glowed incandescently
As if to fulfil their last wish.

The trees bore proudly
This majestic blazing beauty
One last time,
An offering to the Eternal.
Reminiscing the old glory
Of fragrant delicate blossoms.

Then, one by one
The leaves withered,
Descending gently
As if sparkling embers

To fade into oblivion,
Leaving the lush forest
Stark and bare.